Camp
JOURNAL

NAME ....

CONTACTS: ....

....

....

CAMP: ....

DATE: ....

Week

FROM: _____

TO: _____

sunday

activity schedule:

- [ ]
- [ ]
- [ ]

- [ ]
- [ ]
- [ ]

- [ ]
- [ ]
- [ ]

- [ ]
- [ ]
- [ ]

DATE:

Monday

activity schedule:

- [ ] _____
- [ ] _____
- [ ] _____

- [ ] _____
- [ ] _____
- [ ] _____

- [ ] _____
- [ ] _____
- [ ] _____

- [ ] _____
- [ ] _____
- [ ] _____

DATE:

Tuesday

activity schedule:

☐ ------------------------------
☐ ------------------------------
☐ ------------------------------

☐ ------------------------------
☐ ------------------------------
☐ ------------------------------

☐ ------------------------------
☐ ------------------------------
☐ ------------------------------

☐ ------------------------------
☐ ------------------------------
☐ ------------------------------

DATE:
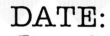

Wednesday

activity schedule:

- [ ] _____
- [ ] _____
- [ ] _____

- [ ] _____
- [ ] _____
- [ ] _____

- [ ] _____
- [ ] _____
- [ ] _____

- [ ] _____
- [ ] _____
- [ ] _____

DATE:

Thursday
activity schedule:

☐ -

☐ -

☐ -

☐ -

☐ -

☐ -

☐ -

☐ -

☐ -

☐ -

☐ -

☐ -

DATE:
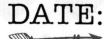

Friday

activity schedule:

☐ -----------------------------------
☐ -----------------------------------
☐ -----------------------------------

☐ -----------------------------------
☐ -----------------------------------
☐ -----------------------------------

☐ -----------------------------------
☐ -----------------------------------
☐ -----------------------------------

☐ -----------------------------------
☐ -----------------------------------
☐ -----------------------------------

DATE:

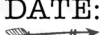

Saturday
activity schedule:

☐ --
☐ --
☐ --

☐ --
☐ --
☐ --

☐ --
☐ --
☐ --

☐ --
☐ --
☐ --

DATE:

Sunday

DATE: _____

DAY'S *highs*

DAY'S *lows*

Monday

DATE:

DAY'S *highs*

DAY'S *lows*

Tuesday

DATE: _____

DAY'S *highs*

DAY'S *lows*

Wednesday

DATE:

DAY'S *highs*

DAY'S *lows*

Thursday

DATE:

DAY'S *highs*

DAY'S *lows*

Friday

DATE: ------------------------

DAY'S *highs*

DAY'S *lows*

saturday

DATE:

DAY'S *highs*

DAY'S *lows*

Skills Learned

Notes:

Drawings

Autographs

Autographs

Week

FROM: _____

TO: _____

Sunday

activity schedule:

☐ --
☐ --
☐ --

☐ --
☐ --
☐ --

☐ --
☐ --
☐ --

☐ --
☐ --
☐ --

DATE:

Monday

activity schedule:

- [ ] _____
- [ ] _____
- [ ] _____

- [ ] _____
- [ ] _____
- [ ] _____

- [ ] _____
- [ ] _____
- [ ] _____

- [ ] _____
- [ ] _____
- [ ] _____

DATE:

Tuesday

activity schedule:

☐ --

☐ --

☐ --

☐ --

☐ --

☐ --

☐ --

☐ --

☐ --

☐ --

☐ --

☐ --

DATE:

Wednesday
activity schedule:

- [ ] _____
- [ ] _____
- [ ] _____

- [ ] _____
- [ ] _____
- [ ] _____

- [ ] _____
- [ ] _____
- [ ] _____

- [ ] _____
- [ ] _____
- [ ] _____

DATE:

Thursday

activity schedule:

☐ --
☐ --
☐ --

☐ --

☐ --

☐ --

☐ --

☐ --

☐ --

☐ --

☐ --

☐ --

DATE:

Friday

activity schedule:

☐ _____
☐ _____
☐ _____

☐ _____
☐ _____
☐ _____

☐ _____
☐ _____
☐ _____

☐ _____
☐ _____
☐ _____

DATE:

saturday

activity schedule:

- ☐
- ☐
- ☐

- ☐
- ☐
- ☐

- ☐
- ☐
- ☐

- ☐
- ☐
- ☐

DATE:

Sunday

DATE: _____

DAY'S *highs*

DAY'S *lows*

Monday

DATE: _____

DAY'S *highs*

DAY'S *lows*

Tuesday

DATE: ---------------------

DAY'S *highs*

DAY'S *lows*

Wednesday

DATE:

DAY'S *highs*

DAY'S *lows*

Thursday

DATE:

DAY'S *highs*

DAY'S *lows*

Friday

DATE:

DAY'S *highs*

DAY'S *lows*

saturday

DATE:

DAY'S *highs*

DAY'S *lows*

skills
Learned

✓ -

✓ -

✓ -

✓ -

✓ -

✓ -

✓ -

- -

Notes:

Drawings

Autographs

Autographs

Week

FROM: _____

TO: _____

sunday

activity schedule:

☐ --
☐ --
☐ --

☐ --
☐ --
☐ --

☐ --
☐ --
☐ --

☐ --
☐ --
☐ --

DATE:

Monday

activity schedule:

- [ ]
- [ ]
- [ ]

- [ ]
- [ ]
- [ ]

- [ ]
- [ ]
- [ ]

- [ ]
- [ ]
- [ ]

DATE:

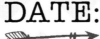

Tuesday

activity schedule:

☐ ------------------------------------
☐ ------------------------------------
☐ ------------------------------------

☐ ------------------------------------
☐ ------------------------------------
☐ ------------------------------------

☐ ------------------------------------
☐ ------------------------------------
☐ ------------------------------------

☐ ------------------------------------
☐ ------------------------------------
☐ ------------------------------------

DATE:

Wednesday

activity schedule:

- [ ] --------------------------------
- [ ] --------------------------------
- [ ] --------------------------------
- [ ] --------------------------------
- [ ] --------------------------------
- [ ] --------------------------------
- [ ] --------------------------------
- [ ] --------------------------------
- [ ] --------------------------------
- [ ] --------------------------------
- [ ] --------------------------------
- [ ] --------------------------------

DATE:

Thursday

activity schedule:

- ☐ ---------------
- ☐ ---------------
- ☐ ---------------

- ☐ ---------------
- ☐ ---------------
- ☐ ---------------

- ☐ ---------------
- ☐ ---------------
- ☐ ---------------

- ☐ ---------------
- ☐ ---------------
- ☐ ---------------

DATE:

Friday

activity schedule:

☐ -------------------------------------

☐ -------------------------------------

☐ -------------------------------------

☐ -------------------------------------

☐ -------------------------------------

☐ -------------------------------------

☐ -------------------------------------

☐ -------------------------------------

☐ -------------------------------------

☐ -------------------------------------

☐ -------------------------------------

☐ -------------------------------------

DATE:

saturday

activity schedule:

☐ --

☐ --

☐ --

☐ --

☐ --

☐ --

☐ --

☐ --

☐ --

☐ --

☐ --

☐ --

DATE:

Sunday

DATE: _ _ _ _ _ _ _ _ _ _

DAY'S *highs*

DAY'S *lows*

Monday

DATE: --------------------

DAY'S *highs*

DAY'S *lows*

Tuesday

DATE:

DAY'S *highs*

DAY'S *lows*

Wednesday

DATE:

DAY'S *highs*

DAY'S *lows*

Thursday

DATE:

DAY'S *highs*

DAY'S *lows*

Friday

DATE:

DAY'S *highs*

DAY'S *lows*

saturday

DATE: _ _ _ _ _ _

DAY'S *highs*

DAY'S *lows*

skills
Learned

Notes:

Drawings

Autographs

Autographs

Week

FROM: _____

TO: _____

sunday

activity schedule:

- [ ]
- [ ]
- [ ]

- [ ]
- [ ]
- [ ]

- [ ]
- [ ]
- [ ]

- [ ]
- [ ]
- [ ]

DATE:

Monday

activity schedule:

☐ --------------------------------
☐ --------------------------------
☐ --------------------------------

☐ --------------------------------
☐ --------------------------------
☐ --------------------------------

☐ --------------------------------
☐ --------------------------------
☐ --------------------------------

☐ --------------------------------
☐ --------------------------------
☐ --------------------------------

DATE:

Tuesday

activity schedule:

- [ ] --
- [ ] --
- [ ] --

- [ ] --
- [ ] --
- [ ] --

- [ ] --
- [ ] --
- [ ] --

- [ ] --
- [ ] --
- [ ] --

DATE:

Wednesday

activity schedule:

☐ ----------------------------------
☐ ----------------------------------
☐ ----------------------------------

☐ ----------------------------------
☐ ----------------------------------
☐ ----------------------------------

☐ ----------------------------------
☐ ----------------------------------
☐ ----------------------------------

☐ ----------------------------------
☐ ----------------------------------
☐ ----------------------------------

DATE:

Thursday
activity schedule:

☐ --

☐ --

☐ --

☐ --

☐ --

☐ --

☐ --

☐ --

☐ --

☐ --

☐ --

☐ --

DATE:

Friday

activity schedule:

- [ ] --------------------------------
- [ ] --------------------------------
- [ ] --------------------------------

- [ ] --------------------------------
- [ ] --------------------------------
- [ ] --------------------------------

- [ ] --------------------------------
- [ ] --------------------------------
- [ ] --------------------------------

- [ ] --------------------------------
- [ ] --------------------------------
- [ ] --------------------------------

DATE:

saturday

activity schedule:

☐ ------------------------------------
☐ ------------------------------------
☐ ------------------------------------

☐ ------------------------------------
☐ ------------------------------------
☐ ------------------------------------

☐ ------------------------------------
☐ ------------------------------------
☐ ------------------------------------

☐ ------------------------------------
☐ ------------------------------------
☐ ------------------------------------

DATE:

Sunday

DATE:

DAY'S *highs*

DAY'S *lows*

Monday

DATE:

DAY'S *highs*

DAY'S *lows*

Tuesday

DATE: _____

DAY'S *highs*

DAY'S *lows*

Wednesday

DATE:

DAY'S *highs*

DAY'S *lows*

Thursday

DATE: _____

DAY'S *highs*

DAY'S *lows*

Friday

DATE: _ _ _ _ _ _ _ _ _

DAY'S *highs*

DAY'S *lows*

Saturday

DATE:

DAY'S *highs*

DAY'S *lows*

Skills Learned

- [x] -
- [x] -
- [x] -
- [x] -
- [x] -
- [x] -
- [x] -

Notes:

Drawings

Autographs

Autographs

new friends:

Name: _____
Phone: _____
Address: _____
Email: _____

Name: _____
Phone: _____
Address: _____
Email: _____

Name: _____
Phone: _____
Address: _____
Email: _____

Name: _____
Phone: _____
Address: _____
Email: _____

Name: _____
Phone: _____
Address: _____
Email: _____

new friends:

Name: _____
Phone: _____
Address: _____
Email: _____

Name: _____
Phone: _____
Address: _____
Email: _____

Name: _____
Phone: _____
Address: _____
Email: _____

Name: _____
Phone: _____
Address: _____
Email: _____

Name: _____
Phone: _____
Address: _____
Email: _____

new friends:

Name: _____
Phone: _____
Address: _____
Email: _____

Name: _____
Phone: _____
Address: _____
Email: _____

Name: _____
Phone: _____
Address: _____
Email: _____

Name: _____
Phone: _____
Address: _____
Email: _____

Name: _____
Phone: _____
Address: _____
Email: _____

new friends:

Name:
Phone:
Address:
Email:

Name:
Phone:
Address:
Email:

Name:
Phone:
Address:
Email:

Name:
Phone:
Address:
Email:

Name:
Phone:
Address:
Email:

new friends:

Name: _____
Phone: _____
Address: _____
Email: _____

Name: _____
Phone: _____
Address: _____
Email: _____

Name: _____
Phone: _____
Address: _____
Email: _____

Name: _____
Phone: _____
Address: _____
Email: _____

Name: _____
Phone: _____
Address: _____
Email: _____

new friends:

Name:
Phone:
Address:
Email:

Name:
Phone:
Address:
Email:

Name:
Phone:
Address:
Email:

Name:
Phone:
Address:
Email:

Name:
Phone:
Address:
Email:

new friends:

Name: _____
Phone: _____
Address: _____
Email: _____

Name: _____
Phone: _____
Address: _____
Email: _____

Name: _____
Phone: _____
Address: _____
Email: _____

Name: _____
Phone: _____
Address: _____
Email: _____

Name: _____
Phone: _____
Address: _____
Email: _____

new friends:

Name:
Phone:
Address:
Email:

Name:
Phone:
Address:
Email:

Name:
Phone:
Address:
Email:

Name:
Phone:
Address:
Email:

Name:
Phone:
Address:
Email:

new *friends:*

Name: _____
Phone: _____
Address: _____
Email: _____

Name: _____
Phone: _____
Address: _____
Email: _____

Name: _____
Phone: _____
Address: _____
Email: _____

Name: _____
Phone: _____
Address: _____
Email: _____

Name: _____
Phone: _____
Address: _____
Email: _____

new friends:

Name:
Phone:
Address:
Email:

Name:
Phone:
Address:
Email:

Name:
Phone:
Address:
Email:

Name:
Phone:
Address:
Email:

Name:
Phone:
Address:
Email:

new friends:

Name: _____
Phone: _____
Address: _____
Email: _____

Name: _____
Phone: _____
Address: _____
Email: _____

Name: _____
Phone: _____
Address: _____
Email: _____

Name: _____
Phone: _____
Address: _____
Email: _____

Name: _____
Phone: _____
Address: _____
Email: _____

new friends:

Name:

Phone:

Address:

Email:

Name:

Phone:

Address:

Email:

Name:

Phone:

Address:

Email:

Name:

Phone:

Address:

Email:

Name:

Phone:

Address:

Email:

new friends:

Name: _____
Phone: _____
Address: _____
Email: _____

Name: _____
Phone: _____
Address: _____
Email: _____

Name: _____
Phone: _____
Address: _____
Email: _____

Name: _____
Phone: _____
Address: _____
Email: _____

Name: _____
Phone: _____
Address: _____
Email: _____

Autographs

Autographs

Autographs

Autographs

Autographs

Made in United States
Orlando, FL
14 June 2022

18803894R00074